Miraculous Magic Tricks

PAPER MAGIC

by Mike Lane
Illustrations by David Mostyn

WINDMILL BOOKS
New York

Published in 2012 by Windmill Books, an Imprint of Rosen Publishing
29 East 21st Street, New York, NY 10010

First Edition

Author: Mike Lane
Editors: Patience Coster and Joe Harris
Illustrations: David Mostyn
Design: Tokiko Morishima

Library of Congress Cataloging-in-Publication Data

Lane, Mike.
Paper magic / by Mike Lane.
p. cm. — (Miraculous magic tricks)
Includes index.
ISBN 978-1-61533-511-4 (library binding) — ISBN 978-1-4488-6729-5 (pbk.) — ISBN 978-1-4488-6730-1 (6-pack)
1. Magic tricks. 2. Paper. I. Title.
GV1547.L285 2012
793.8—dc23
2011021766

Printed in China

CPSIA Compliance Information: Batch # AW2102WM: For further information contact Windmill Books, New York, New York at 1-866-478-0556

SL002050US

CONTENTS

INTRODUCTION

Within these pages you will discover great paper tricks that are easy to do and impressive to watch.

To be a successful magician, you will need to practice the tricks in private before you perform them in front of an audience. An excellent way to practice is in front of a mirror, since you can watch the magic happen before your own eyes.

When performing, you must speak clearly, slowly, and loudly enough for everyone to hear. But never tell the audience what's going to happen.

Remember to "watch your angles." This means being careful about where your spectators are standing or sitting when you are performing. The best place is directly in front of you.

Never tell the secret of how the trick is done. If someone asks, just say: "It's magic!"

THE MAGICIAN'S PLEDGE

I promise not to reveal the secrets of magic to those who are not magicians.

I promise to practice these magic tricks over and over again before attempting to perform them in front of an audience.

I promise to respect my art, the art of magic.

STEPPING THROUGH PAPER

ILLUSION

The magician holds up a letter-sized sheet of paper. He tells the spectator he will cut a hole in the paper big enough to step through, and he does.

1 The magician folds the paper in half lengthwise.

2 Starting approximately ½ inch (1 cm) down from the top edge, the magician cuts in a straight line from the crease to the open edge, stopping just before the edge. He must be careful NOT to cut right across!

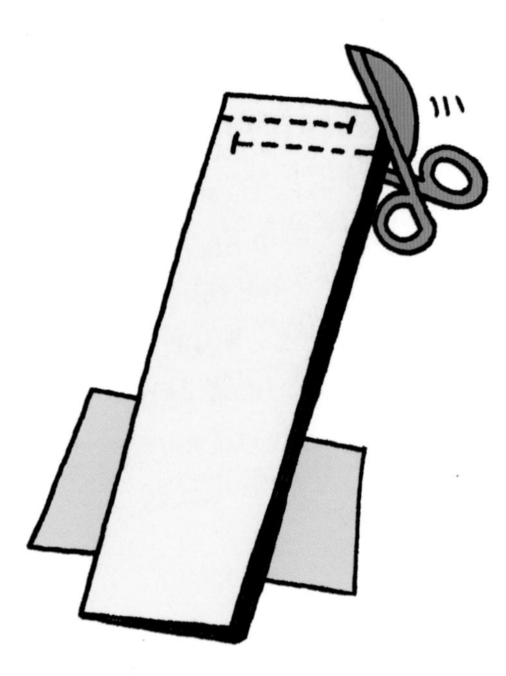

3 Now he makes a second cut from the open edge toward the crease, starting ½ inch (1 cm) below the first cut and stopping just before the crease in the same way.

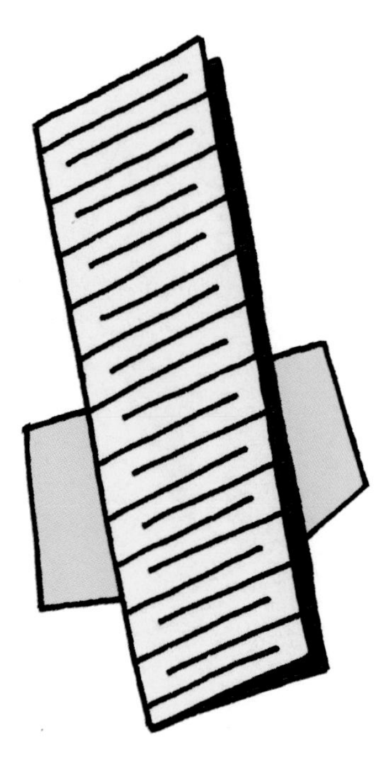

4 He continues this back and forth, cutting until he reaches ½ inch (1 cm) from the bottom edge of the paper.

5 Once he has finished cutting, he opens the page carefully. He now cuts all the folds down the spine of the page APART from those at the top and the bottom.

6 The paper should now form a large circle. The magician carefully steps through the hole in the paper.

MAGICAL MEND

ILLUSION

The magician cuts a column of print from a newspaper, folds it, cuts it, and then restores it to its uncut form.

1 Prior to the trick, the magician prepares the newspaper by cutting out a long column of print.

2 He sticks the two ends of a piece of adhesive tape together to make a loop, then sticks it in the middle of the back of the column. The spectator will not see this reverse side of the paper.

3 To perform the trick, the magician holds the newspaper column up so that the spectator sees the front of it.

4 The magician folds the newspaper column in half from top to bottom. He folds it toward himself so that the tape holds the two surfaces together.

 With a pair of scissors, he cuts the folded newspaper just under the fold but not ON it.

6 The magician holds the bottom edge of the paper, and folds the other half up toward the audience. Because the tape is holding the two sides together, it will appear that the paper is still in one piece.

FLOATING CUP

ILLUSION

The magician holds a cup in his hands. He lets go of it slowly and it remains floating in mid-air.

1 Prior to the trick, the magician takes a large paper or foam cup and pokes a hole halfway up with his thumb.

2 To perform the trick, he picks up the cup with both hands, with the hole facing him.

3 He wraps his fingers round the sides of the cup and inserts a thumb into the hole from behind.

4 The magician now loosens his grip and slowly wiggles his fingers close to the cup. From the spectator's side it will look as though the cup is floating. The magician must be sure the spectator cannot see the cup from behind.

5 The magician once again grips the cup with his fingers, removes his thumb from the hole, and puts the cup aside.

PAPER JUMP

ILLUSION

A small piece of paper taped to the magician's fingernail jumps back and forth between two fingers.

1 Prior to this trick, the magician tapes a small piece of paper to the nail of his middle finger.

2 The magician places his middle and index fingers of this hand on the edge of a table with the thumb and remaining fingers curled under.

3 The magician lifts the fingers to his shoulder, curls in his index finger, and sticks out his ring finger. This movement is done quickly.

4 The magician brings his fingers back down to the edge of the table.The spectators will be amazed as it will look as though the paper has jumped from one finger to the other.

MAGIC TIP!

THIS TRICK CAN BE REPEATED OVER AND OVER, MAKING IT LOOK AS THOUGH THE PAPER IS JUMPING BACK AND FORTH. THE QUICKER IT IS DONE, THE BETTER IT LOOKS.

5 The magician lifts his hand to his shoulder again. Switching his fingers back to the starting position, he brings them back down onto the table.

A TREE FROM PAPER

ILLUSION
Making a tree from a sheet of newspaper, just for fun!

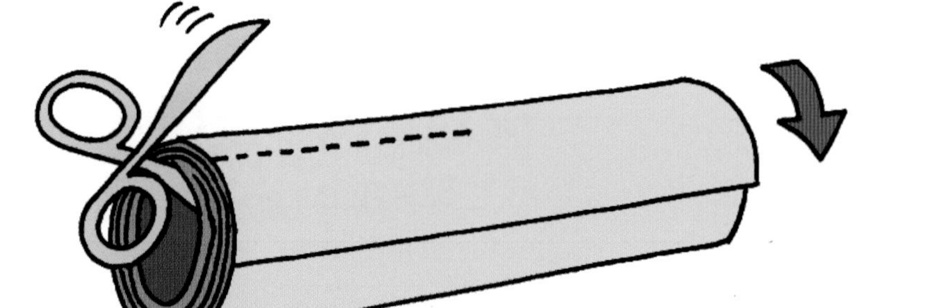

1 The magician takes a sheet of newspaper and rolls it into a tube.

2 With a pair of scissors, he cuts a slit from the top of one side to about halfway down.

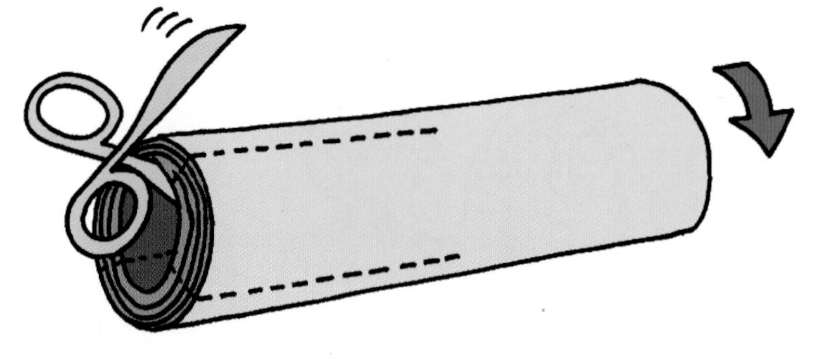

3 He does this twice more, keeping the space between the slits equal.

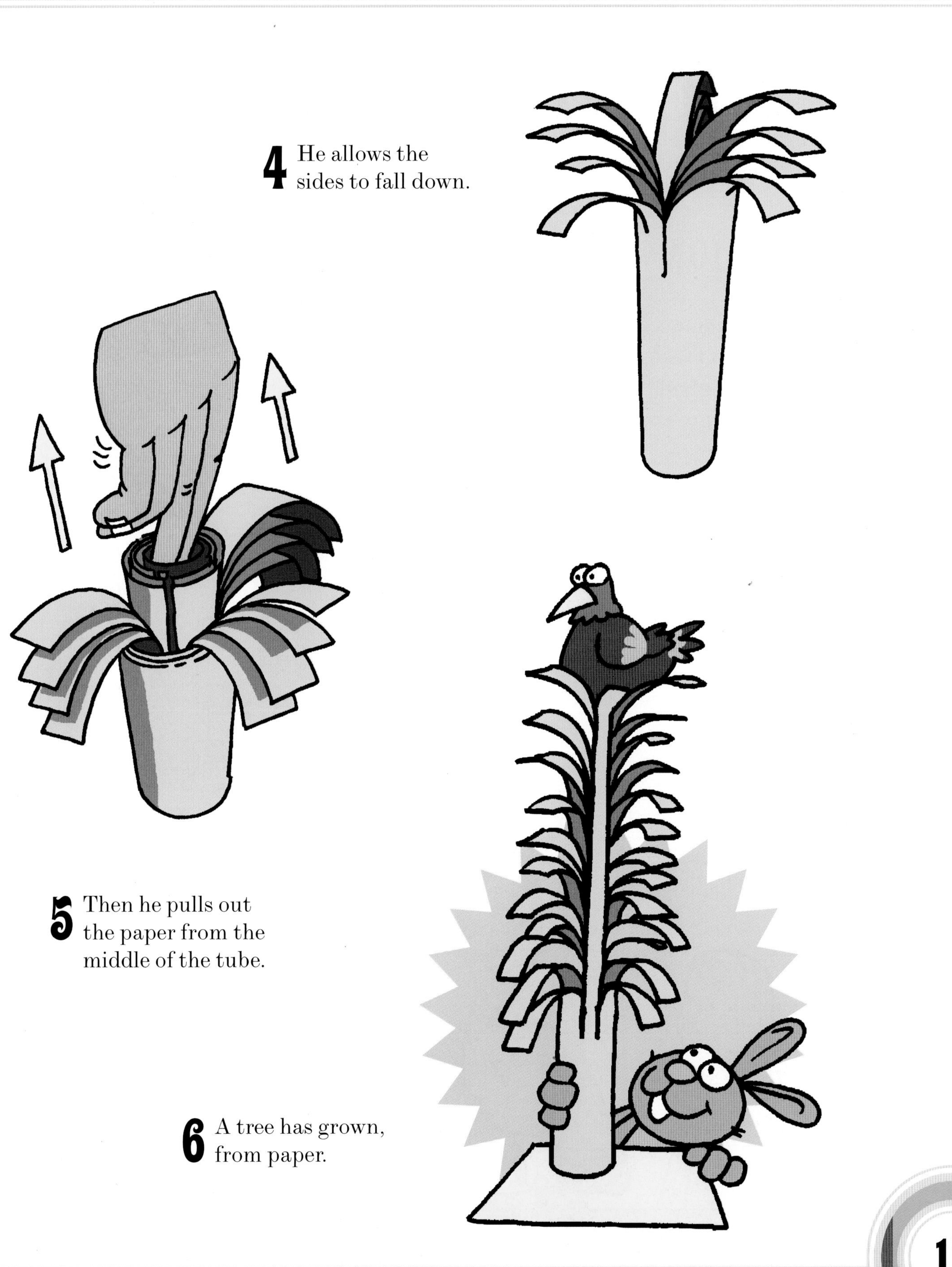

4 He allows the sides to fall down.

5 Then he pulls out the paper from the middle of the tube.

6 A tree has grown, from paper.

OVERHEAD

ILLUSION

A spectator is seated facing the audience. The magician makes several paper balls disappear before the spectator's eyes.

1 The magician asks a spectator to sit on a chair facing the audience.

2 The magician rolls up a paper tissue into a ball and shows it to the spectator and the audience.

3 The magician throws the tissue ball from hand to hand in front of the spectator.

4 The magician now quickly tosses the tissue ball over the spectator's head, but continues to act as though the ball is still going back and forth between both hands. Of course, the audience will see the tissue go over the spectator's head.

MAGIC TIP!
KEEP REPEATING THIS TRICK OVER AND OVER UNTIL THE SPECTATOR FINALLY CATCHES ON!

5 The magician now opens his hands and shows the puzzled spectator that the tissue ball has vanished.

MONEY MORPH

ILLUSION
A bill of one value is folded and changes (morphs) into a bill of different value when it is unfolded.

1 Prior to the trick, the magician takes two bills of different value and places one of them on a table.

2 He folds this bill in half from left to right.

3 Then he folds it in half again from left to right.

4 Now he folds it in half a third time, from top to bottom, to form a square.

5 He places the second bill on the table.

6 With a piece of sticky tape, he attaches the folded bill to the bottom right-hand corner of the second bill, with the creased side uppermost. The folded bill should be completely hidden behind the second bill.

7 The magician is now ready to perform. He holds up the bill for the spectators to see. The magician's right thumb covers the folded bill at the back and his fingers are held in front of the second bill. He holds the left-hand side of the bill with his left hand.

8 The magician folds the bill in half from left to right.

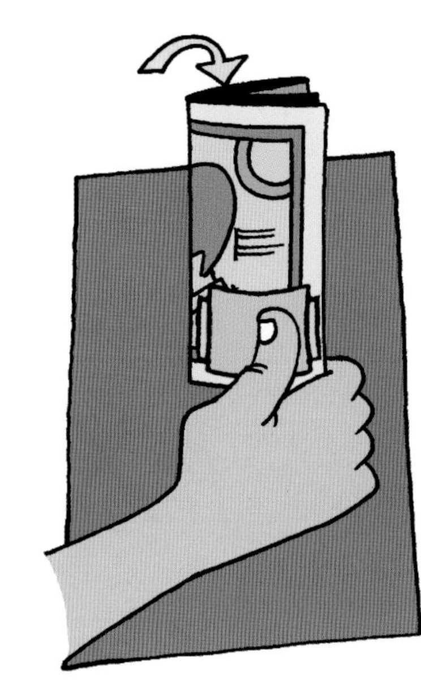

9 He folds it in half again the same way.

10 Then he folds it in half a third time, from top to bottom, being careful not to expose the hidden bill.

11 The magician quickly flips the bills over so that the back bill becomes the front bill and the front bill becomes the back bill.

12 Using both hands, he carefully unfolds the front bill (which was the back bill), being careful not to expose the back bill (which was the front bill). His hands should be in the same position as when the trick began.

TIC TAC TOE

ILLUSION

Three pieces of paper, two marked with an X and one marked with an O, are dropped into a bag. With his eyes closed, the magician can pick out any piece the spectator calls out.

1 On a sheet of paper, the magician draws a large X followed by a large O and then a large X. Each letter should take up one third of the page.

2 The magician folds the paper into three.

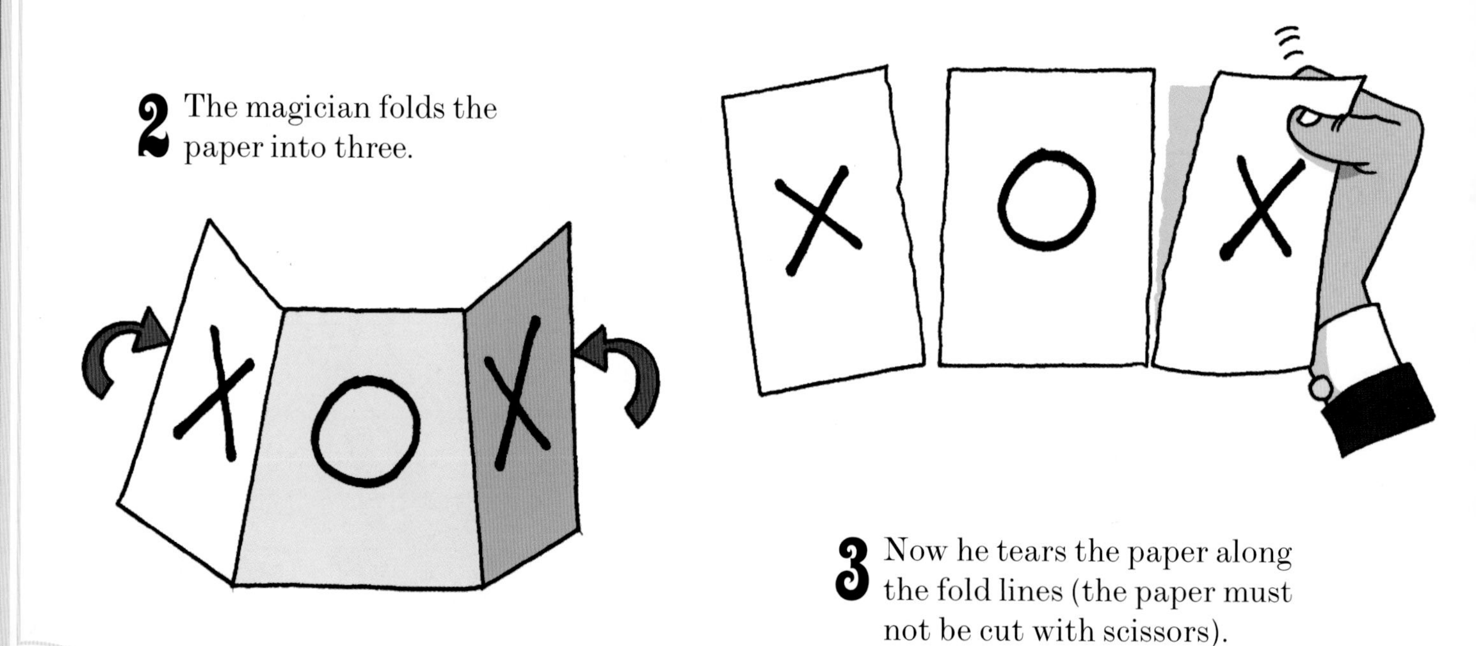

3 Now he tears the paper along the fold lines (the paper must not be cut with scissors).

MAGIC TIP!
THE MAGICIAN CAN WEAR A BLINDFOLD TO ADD EXTRA DRAMA TO THE TRICK.

4 The magician places the three pieces of paper in a bag and asks a spectator to call out "O" or "X."

5 The magician reaches into the bag and removes whichever letter is called out. He does this by feeling the edges of the long sides of the paper: the X pieces have one smooth, straight side and one torn side; the O piece has two torn sides.

RIP IT, RESTORE IT

ILLUSION

The magician shows the audience a page from a newspaper or magazine and proceeds to rip it into several pieces. He squeezes the pieces into a ball, unfolds the ball, and the paper is back in one piece.

1. Prior to the trick, the magician takes two duplicate pages from a newspaper or magazine. He crumples one page into a ball.

2. The magician hides the crumpled page behind the other page, holding it with his thumb against the top left-hand corner. He holds his fingers in front of the page, visible to the spectators.

3 With his right hand, the magician starts ripping the page into strips. Each time a strip is ripped, he places it in front of the area where the crumpled ball is hidden.

4 Once several strips have been ripped, the magician squeezes them together using both hands. He must be careful not to combine the ripped pieces with the pre-crumpled ball. At this point, there should be two paper balls in the magician's hands.

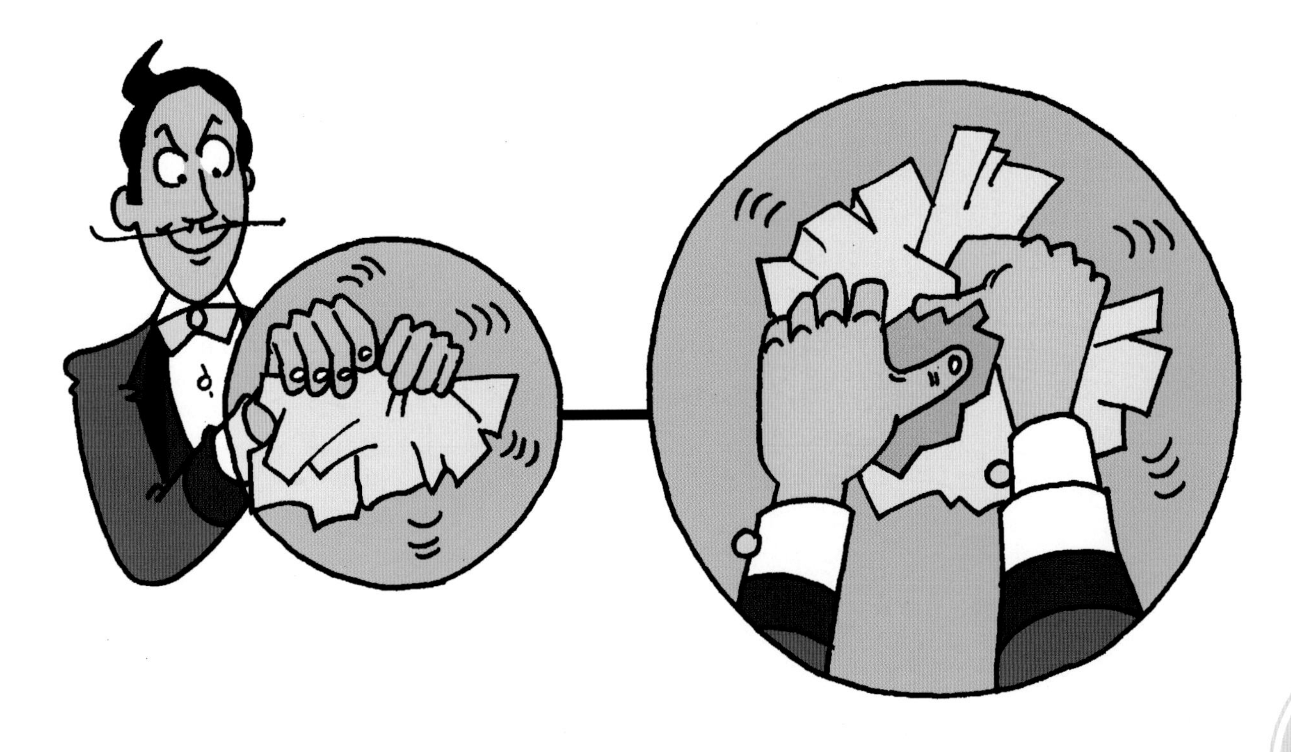

5 The magician takes the paper balls in his right hand.

6 The ball of un-ripped paper should be on top.

7 Slowly, the magician opens his hand and, keeping the ripped ball hidden, begins to unfold the un-ripped ball. He hides the ripped ball behind the open page, which appears to have been magically restored.

PSYCHIC PAPER

ILLUSION

The magician attempts to read the spectator's minds while they are thinking of an item. The magician writes down the item he believes they are thinking of. At first, the spectators think the magician has failed, but he proves at the end of the trick that he got them all correct.

1 The magician needs four spectators to assist with this trick. One of them is secretly part of the trick. Before the trick, the magician tells his secret assistant to say "apples" in answer to his question.

2 The magician has a pen, a pad, and a clear plastic bag. He asks a spectator (not his secret assistant, who will be fourth) to silently think of an item from a grocery store. He acts as if he is reading the spectator's mind and writes down the word "apples."

3 The magician asks the spectator what item they were thinking of. Let's imagine that they say "milk." The magician looks disappointed, rips the page from the pad, and crumples it into a ball. He puts the ball in the plastic bag. He does not show the spectators what he wrote before crumpling the page into a ball.

4 The magician now turns to the second spectator. He tells them to: "Think of an item and look into my eyes." He writes down the item the first spectator said (in our example, "milk"). The magician asks the second spectator what their item was (let's say it was "bread"). Again the magician looks disappointed, rips out the page from the pad, crumples it into a ball, and throws it in the plastic bag.

5 The magicians now asks the third spectator the same question. He writes down the item the second spectator said (in our example, "bread"). Once again the magician asks what the item was (let's say it was"toothpaste"). He again looks disappointed, rips, crumples, and tosses the page into the bag.

6 Finally, the magician asks his secret assistant to think of an item. He writes down the item the third spectator said (in our example,"toothpaste"). He asks the secret assistant what the item was. Of course the item will be apples. Once again the magician, rips, crumples, and tosses the page into the bag.

7 The magician now announces,"I never said I got the answers wrong!" He removes the crumpled balls from the bag, opens them up, and shows the spectators that he had indeed written down each of the items they had thought of.

FURTHER READING

Barnhart, Norm. *Amazing Magic Tricks.* Mankato, MN: Capstone Press, 2008.

Charney, Steve. *Amazing Tricks with Everyday Stuff.* Mankato, MN: Capstone Press, 2011.

Charney, Steve. *Incredible Tricks at the Dinner Table.* Mankato, MN: Capstone Press, 2011.

Klingel, Cynthia. *Magic Tricks.* Mankato, MN: Compass Point Books, 2002.

Longe, Bob. *Classic Magic Tricks.* New York, NY: Metro Books, 2002.

Tremaine, Jon. *Instant Magic.* Hauppauge, NY: Barron's Educational Series, 2009.

WEB SITES

For Web resources related to the subject of this book, go to: www.windmillbooks.com/weblinks and select this book's title.

GLOSSARY

audience (AH-dee-ints) A group of people who watch or listen to something.
morph (MORF) To change in shape or form.
pledge (PLEJ) A promise or agreement.
prior (PRY-ur) Before or ahead of.
spectator (SPEK-tay-ter) A person who sees or watches something.
wiggles (WIH-gels) Makes small movements.

INDEX